Tove Jensen Holmås & Stig Holmås

BERGEN

SKALD 2007

Photos: Robin Strand, p. 4, 7, 10, 14, 22, 25, 30, 33, 34, 36, 40, 48, 52, 57, 59, 60, 62, 64, 66, 69, 70, 74, 77, 78, 80, 82, 84, 86, 89, 90, 92, 95 Chris Kyllingmark p. 8, Knud Knudsen p. 12, 46, Knut Strand p. 15, 21, 94, Helge Sunde p. 32, Arne Nilsen p. 43, Oddleiv Apneseth p. 44, 53 Helge Hansen p. 75, Håvard Bjelland p. 76, Universitetet i Bergen, Billedsamlingen p. 26, 28, 39, 73, Hansa p. 17, Bergen Kommune p. 20 Kirsten Hetland p. 18, Arne Barlindhaug Ellingsen p. 35, 42, 51, 68, Magnus Vabø p. 54, Teaterarkivet, UiB p. 72

Cover photos: Robin Strand

English translation: Kjersti Riise

Graphic design: Silje Nes/Arne Barlindhaug Ellingsen
Printed in Kaunas, Lithuania

© SKALD AS 2007

Tel: +47 57 65 41 55
e-mail: forlag@skald.no
www.skald.no

ISBN 978-82-7959-100-9 (norsk utgåve)
ISBN 978-827959-088-0 (English edition)
ISBN 978-82-7959-104-7 (Deutsche Ausgabe)

CONTENTS

BERGEN AND ITS PEOPLE

Situated on the coast, at the foot of mountains and shielded from the sea by a large island, lies Bergen, Norway's most attractive city. Innermost in Vågen, Bergen's oldest port, we find Fisketorget, the town's famous fish market. Cafes lie side by side along the quays. On the east side of Vågen is Bryggen, a unique collection of wooden houses with gables facing the harbour. Bryggen's architecture has remained the same for hundreds of years and is on UNESCO's World Heritage List.

Bergen is one of Europe's best preserved wooden cities. It has steep stairways and narrow cobblestone alleys between old wooden houses painted in white. Up on the mountainside, villas and apartment buildings cling to the edge. Amongst them, on steep rails, a blue carriage rolls toward its final destination on the mountain called Fløien. Halfway up it passes its twin red carriage on its way down. A bit later they meet again, the blue one on its way down and the red on its way up. From the top of Fløien the view is phenomenal.

Bergen is a beautifully placed gem; a blooming and modern cultural city with a very special history. We who live here are proud to show our town to others.

Bergen is positioned at 60° 23' 36 N, 5° 23' 18 N. These are the coordinates of the Bergen Dome Church spire.

Winter on Bryggen.

Ships from several eras.

THE TIME OF THE VIKINGS

The streets of Bergen are steeped in the past, and although it is not a big city, having roughly 250,000 inhabitants, you will find that it has a certain urban European flavour. Since its foundation, Bergen has looked west and out towards the world. This is where the majority of inhabitants and cultural impulses stem from, and the street and alley names tell their tales: Hollendergaten: the street of the Dutch, Skottegaten: the street of the Scots and Tyskesmauet: the German alley.

None of us know the exact age of our town. The Norwegian king Olav Kyrre was given the honour of founding Bergen in the year 1070, but we know that people lived and traded here long before that time.

In the 8th and 9th centuries, fearless seamen – the so called Vikings, sailed from places north and south of Bergen – all the way to Scotland, Eng-

THE VIKINGS

The word Viking was used to describe Scandinavian seamen from about 800-1050. The Vikings were both tradesmen and warriors. They sailed across the sea westwards as far as North America, southwards to the Mediterranean, eastwards deep into Russia, and further along great rivers as far as the Black Sea, Baghdad and the Caspian Sea. The Viking ships had single masts and were open, clinker-built vessels. They sailed or rowed with many pairs of oars.

land and Ireland. They travelled west over the ocean in open boats, discovered new lands and settled there – in the Faroe Islands, Iceland and Greenland. From Greenland the Viking Leiv Erikson sailed westwards and reached North America – about 500 years before Christopher Columbus was stranded on the island he called San Salvador.

During the time of the Vikings, there were two farms between the mountains in Bergendalen (Bergen Valley). One was the king's farm Alrekstad, and the other was called Bjargvin. The latter means the plain between the mountains, and is the origin of the present name Bergen. The people who lived on these two farms had slipways, boat-houses and quays innermost in Vågen near the place where the fish market now lies.

STOCK FISH TOWN

After Olav Kyrre gave Bergen the status of «market town» the town grew rapidly. It became a kingdom, a diocese, and after a while more monasteries and convents came into existence. At the same time Bergen became Norway's most important centre for shipping and foreign trade. As early as the time of Olav Kyrre, English merchant ships came to Bergen. Later, from the second half of the 12th century, trade with Germans became more and more important.

Why did foreigners come to Bergen? What did they have to offer? What did they take with them when they left? Englishmen brought flour, honey, wax, textiles and copper kettles. Germans came with rye and wine, amongst other things. At the end of the 12th century, Norway became dependent on the import of corn. Bergen had exclusive ownership of corn import, and thereby a national monopoly on bread. This also contributed to strengthening the city's standing abroad.

Most important of all was the product that the town itself offered, namely skrei, the Northern Norwegian variety of cod, or more correctly, the Stock fish. Stock fish is skrei which is cut and cleaned, and dried in the wind on big racks called «hjell» on the coast of Northern Norway. This method of preservation created foodstuffs perfect for people in the warm Mediterranean. Bergen became a junction between the rich fishing grounds in the scattered communities of Northern Norway and the big markets in Southern Europe. Stock fish trade became the main reason for the town's growth. For centuries Bergen was Scandinavia's most important exporting town. Even though Oslo became the capital of Norway in 1299, Bergen remained the country's biggest town until the end of the 19th century.

The people of Bergen were not very involved with their capital city. They focused on the north and the west instead.

When the fish had dried for several months on the racks in the north,

Bryggen and Vågen in the 1880s.

the fishermen took their cargo of dried fish southwards to the businessmen in Bergen. The freight was sent by sea in Northern Norwegian vessels called «jekter». A jekt was a broad and open wooden boat with one mast, between 40 and 50 feet long. It was loaded with Stock fish. Sailing time from the North of Norway to Bergen could vary between seven and fourteen days.

Seamen from the North came to Bergen twice during the summer months, and hundreds of jekter could be seen in Vågen. The men also brought other

merchandise – cod-liver oil, skins and dried halibut. Sometimes the jekter were so close together that people could walk across Vågen without getting wet. During these visits the town was bursting with life and the sound of creaking derricks. The men from the North had work to do, other than the loading and unloading of boats. There were sails to be fixed or replaced, ropes to be mended, and damaged masts and hulls to be repaired. This generated work for a great deal of the Bergen's inhabitants. When the Northerners

REJECTING

After the Stock fish was unloaded, its quality was checked and it was classified. This was called rejecting, and those doing it were rejecters. A rejecter would have to be familiar with different customer demands concerning length, weight and quality. The fish was divided into a long list of different classes.

headed home their boats were loaded with wood, grains, flour, sugar, and believe it or not, coffins. Along the northern coast, wood was in short supply. It's said that the coffins were filled with biscuits and liquor.

Stock fish was Bergen's most important export throughout nearly the entire history of the town's existence. At the end of the 18th century, the advance from sails to steam meant that the people of the North slowly stopped coming. They shipped their fish to Bergen by steamboat instead. Nevertheless, until recently the city remained the «Stock fish city». Periodically Bergen also exported klippfisk - split, salted and dried cod. Whenever anyone in the world enjoyed stockafisso, estocaficada, bacalao or bacalhau, the commodities had definitely dropped by Bergen before reaching pots and pans in Rome, Nice, Madrid or Lisbon.

Stock fish. In the 19th century the export of fish diminished in Bergen. Today most of the stock fish export is done directly from the north of Norway.

⊃ Bergen's got a large umbrella consumption.

THE RAIN

«It rains way too much in Bergen», other Norwegians say. People from Bergen have decided to like the rain. We don't really have a choice. You can't live in a town like ours and hate rain. Otherwise you'd be miserable more than 230 days a year. We've accepted it and included it into the long list of sights and landmarks making us patriots. «It rains more here than any other town in Norway», the «man from Bergen» exclaims proudly.

The weather has always been an important part of the shipping town Bergen. People were engaged in whether the wind would come from the north or south, and whether or not there was a storm coming. It's no coincidence that some of the world's most groundbreaking meteorologists lived in Bergen. It has been rumoured that one of them described the «man from Bergen» as being extremely preoccupied by the weather, as he «regarded it as his local speciality.»

THE HANSEATIC LEAGUE

Throughout the centuries Bergen has traded with several countries; but none has influenced the city as much as Germany.

Their merchant ships had been anchoring in Bergen since the 11th century, and in the mid-12th century the German merchants started spending their winters on Bryggen («The Wharf»). A union of traders called «The Hanseatic League» flourished in Flanders and Germany, and in the mid-13th century a branch was developed in Bergen. They settled here, and after a short while gained control over the old quarter on the east side of Vågen, including Bryggen.

The Hanseatic League influenced the city's commerce for a couple of hundred years before losing power in the 16th century. However, the Hanseatic branch called the Office was not liquidated until 1754, and the city's oldest contemporary church, Mariakirken (church of St. Mary), held sermons in German right up until 1868.

The Germans were not the only immigrants in Bergen. At the end of the Hanseatic golden age another wave of foreigners arrived to seek their fortunes. They were craftsmen, merchants, brokers, captains, sailors, manual workers and adventurers. Most of them were from Germany, but some were from Denmark, England and Scotland, as well as a considerable amount from Holland. Immigration lasted several hundred years and at one point people born in Norway were probably in the minority. Among those were sons and descendants of people from other countries.

At the end of the 17th century, immigration had decreased, but it had left its mark on the city. At the start of the 18th century, Bergen's five richest families had foreign names. In the 19th century Bergen's population increased yet again, but this time due to people originally from the districts north and south of the city. Almost none were from Oslo. The contact between Bergen – the city of Stock fish – and the capital remained minimal.

With the inclusion of four of the neighbouring municipalities in 1972, Bergen doubled in size.

Immigration has increased during the last decades. Our new fellow citizens come from places more distant than before. Our five largest groups of immigrants originate from Iraq, Vietnam, Chile, Sri Lanka and Great Britain. Immigrants constitute 8 % of the city's population. Bergen has more flavours than ever before.

~~~

HANSA BREWERY

Bergen's connection with the Hanseatic League has given name to the city's brewery: «Hansa bryggeri A/S». The company with its present name has existed since 1891, as an extension of a brewery built in 1849. The tasty Hansa beer, its pale ale in particular, is popular all over the country.

BERGENSEREN – THE MAN FROM BERGEN

In 1737 the native poet Ludvig Holberg compared the city to Noah's ark, describing it as a place for gathering all living creatures.

Trading and great immigration from Europe gave Bergen an urban quality. The inhabitants were urbanites and Europeans. The Germans had long had their own districts and habits, as had the Dutch, Brits and Scots. Gradually they mixed and married, but it wasn't until immigration decreased at the end of the 17th century that «the man from Bergen» – «Bergenseren» gradually came into existence. Prior to this the city was split into different cultures – languages, nationalities and customs.

It's obviously difficult to describe the mood of all the inhabitants of a city collectively, but if we are to believe the general opinion of others, the average man from Bergen is not particularly modest and is rarely quiet. He is known for his quick replies, endless nagging and long, grandiose speeches. In other words he loves to talk, and loudly at that. Why? It has more than likely got something to do with foreign influences, the Hanseatic times or the enterprising immigrants who invaded the city from the European continent, and the factors that will continue to characterize it for many days to come. While most Norwegians are relatively soft-spoken, the people from Bergen are, with their European ancestry, louder. The city certainly had a lot of languages fighting for attention. The history of the loud voices of Bergen can be traced back to the days when the people of the town met up at the fish market; days where haggling and bargaining were mandatory parts of everyday market trade. Throughout history, Bergen has undoubtedly been a noisy city. Wagons rattled through the streets and barrels of herring and dried cod were wheeled alongside the quays. The derricks creaked as the large trading vessels were loaded and unloaded. Since then, cranes and lorries have replaced the derricks and wagons. During a certain period, the trams clattered through the town centre, a somewhat clamorous event! In order to be heard in all this noise, voices needed to be raised, and as mentioned earlier, a lot of languages were fighting for attention.

«Nothing», the Norwegian author Jakob Sande (not from Bergen) said, «nothing is more quiet than a dead man from Bergen.»

The Bergenser is renowned for his patriotism. Some would claim that it is narrow-minded local nationalism.

«I'm not from Norway, I'm from Bergen» is an established Bergen motto. They say it with a smile though, because they're not fighting for a sovereign state or waging war against their own countrymen: they just feel special.

The boys of Bergen drawn by the artist Audun Hetland.

They've got their own flag and their own song, which is performed standing, and much more frequently than the Norwegian national anthem. As an apparent paradox: No place in Norway celebrates the 17th of May, the national day, with greater joy and flying colours than Bergen. The national day procession is a grand mix of tasteful parades and wild carnival gigs. The song of Bergen is a customary part of these celebrations. No one in Bergen finds that odd. The song was written in 1791 by a bishop originally from Trøndelag (a region north of Bergen) and was called «Udsigter fra Ulriken» - views from Ulriken. A distinctive feature of Bergen is that it doesn't take long for people living here to call themselves «Bergenser» no matter where they originated. Those seeking assimilation need not worry; to be a «Bergenser» is not a question of origin or genes, it's more a question of attitude.

Nothing is as typically «Bergensk» as the «kjuagutten», a well-known feature and common denominator for the sharp-tongued and streetwise youths of Bergen. Being considered a «kjuagutt» here in Bergen is, in fact, the greatest of all honours. These days «boys» of all age groups, from 0 to 100 can bear this title. However, in order to be a genuine carrier of this title, one ought really to have been a member of a so called «buekorps» – a phenomenon in Bergen found by outsiders to be the strangest of all.

THE COAT OF ARMS

Bergen's coat of arms is a more recent version of the city's old seal, mentioned for the first time in 1293. Bergen was the first town in Norway to have its own seal. Today the coat of arms is used on official letters and documents, and on the town's flag. The coat of arms consists of a circle with a red base, framed in gold. There is a three towered fortress inside the circle covering seven ridges in gold. Bergen is known for its position surrounded by seven mountains.

⇨ *Hip-hip hooray!*

⇨⇨ *View from Ulriken.*

THE BUEKORPS – BERGEN'S MARCHING YOUTH

Nowadays, a mere 20 «buekorps» exist in Bergen. Once upon a time, there were a great deal more.

The Buekorps are organised groups of boys, and in later years girls, which dress up in uniforms each spring and gather neatly behind their respective banners. These corps are organised as military groups consisting of officers, drummers and soldiers. The officers carry sables and the soldiers have rifles and wooden bow-like weaponry, both of which are useless as firearms. Although they are as harmless as Boy Scouts, the Buekorps often stir negative and head-shaking reactions among other Norwegian citizens. In Bergen however, they are fondly appreciated by many.

The Buekorps as we know it came into existence in the middle of the 19th century. Those were the days when citizens, tradesmen and craftsmen had to serve in the civil army - a semi-military organisation held as a reserve force in case of war. The civil army also had the duty of fighting fires. The «kjuagutter» would often watch as the civil army practiced and performed, and for fun they would imitate their heroes and create their own copies of the armed companies. This is how the «buekorps» started. The different companies we see proudly marching through the streets and alleys of Bergen today represent different areas in Bergen. The older regions close to the city centre have their own corps bearing the name of the region they represent. Nordnæs Bataillon, Skutevikens Buekorps and Laksevågs Bueskyttere are three examples. The sound of the buekorps drums from streets, alleys and open spaces is a sure sign of spring in Bergen.

Buekorps-boys.

Extinguishing of the fire at Bryggen in 1955.

THE FIRES - THE CURSE OF THE CITY

The first building site to develop in Bergen was on the east side of Vågen. It stretched from Korskirken, the church of the Cross, in the south out to Holmen in the north. This is where the royal palace was built, and the bishop lived there. There was also a Dominican monastery, and the king had his residence in Bergen until 1299.

Close to the royal palace at Holmen, known today as The fortress of Bergenhus, are two of the city's most famous buildings – Haakon's hall and Rosenkrantz tower. On the outcrop east of Bergenhus is another fortress, Sverresborg. It was built in 1185 by one of Norway's most famous kings, Sverre Sigurdson. The main part of the city was to be found south of Holmen between Vågen in the west and Langestretet in the east. Langestretet (today Øvregaten and lille Øvregaten) is the oldest street in Bergen and probably also in Norway.

Most of Bergen's population lived in this area, and all of the buildings were made of wood. The buildings and inhabitants suffered many fires – and ever since Bergen's foundation, these fires have been known as «the curse of the city of wooden houses».

From the 12th century, buildings started to develop at Strandsiden (beachside) on the west side of Vågen. Prior to that there were two churches, two convents and the archbishop's palace. Building escalated in the 13th century, and the merchants of Bergen, the rivals of the Hanseatic League, settled there. Unfortunately, this part of town was also ravaged by fires.

Practically all of the fires occurred during the north wind. It drove the flames from one house to the next. Wind from the south or southwest brings rain. Bergen is not only the city of fire, but also of rain.

The town squares reaching from the east to the west were created as firebreaks to prevent the flames from spreading.

These are the years of the big town fires in Bergen: 1170, 1198, 1248, 1332, 1393, 1413, 1429, 1476, 1489, 1527, 1561, 1582, 1589, 1623, 1640, 1660, 1675, 1686, 1702, 1751, 1756, 1771, 1780, 1795, 1800, 1830, 1855, 1901, 1916, 1925, 1930, 1940, 1944, 1955.

After the 1916 fire which destroyed the west side of Vågen, a large part of the burnt down blocks were rebuilt in brick. The southernmost blocks were left standing. Further north along Vågen at Nordnes, most of the wooden buildings were destroyed during the Second World War.

Even though Bergen was often ruined by fires, it was rebuilt in its original style. The buildings did not survive the fires, but the architecture and the medieval building techniques did. The Hanseatic League was the most traditional. After the 1702 fire, the architecture of Bryggen was reconstructed to more or less the same medieval style it had before it was laid in ashes by the fire.

BRYGGEN AND THE HANSA AGE

Bryggen («The Wharf»), made the UNESCO world heritage list in 1980. Before the fire of 1702 there were more wooden buildings than there are today, their fronts reaching from Vetrelidsallmenning in the south to Dreggensallmenning in the north. Some of the buildings were destroyed by fire again in

~~~

THE BLACK PLAGUE

The great plague which devastated Asia and Europe arrived in Bergen in 1349 by ship from Europe. From here the disease spread throughout the country. Just over a third of the population survived.

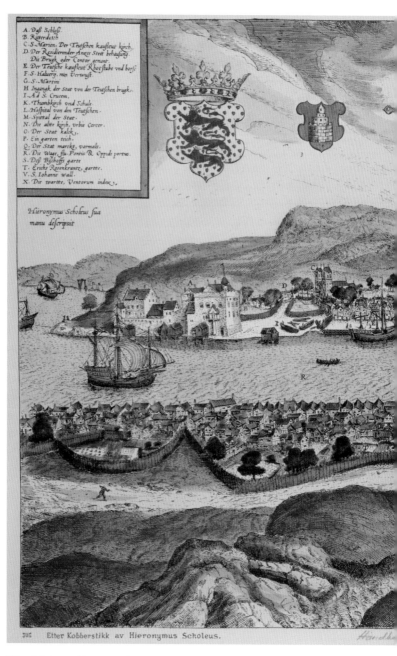

Hieronymus Scholeus sua
manu descripsit

Etter Kobberstikk av Hieronymus Scholeus.

The «Scholeus-stikk» from 1580 – the oldest known picture of Bergen.

1955. Six of them were rebuilt with the original fronts as part of the present SAS-hotel.

At Bryggen there's a strong sensation of the city's history; the same wooden houses are standing from hundreds of years ago, and the smell of tar and Stock fish still lingers in the wooden walls.

Stukket av Franciscus Hogenberg, ca. 1580.

Bergen's oldest settlement was at Bryggen. In the beginning, the method of construction was simple framework. Later on log building became more widespread. Archaeological excavations revealed settlements at Bryggen from the first part of the 11th century. The uncovered building pattern has mostly been preserved. This pattern is distinguished by long continuous rows

THE GAMES – THE CRUEL INITIATION RITUALS OF THE HANSEATIC LEAGUE

Whenever new apprentices arrived in Bergen from Germany to join and serve the Hanseatic League they would have to undergo various unofficial initiation rituals. These rituals were called games, but could be quite uncomfortable and painful. The rawness and intensity of the games increased in the 15th century as the Hansa wished to exclude sons of wealthy German families from competition for Bergen trade. The games, having features of carnivals and processions, drew heaps of spectators, but were deadly serious for the central characters. They could be soiled by tar and faeces, hung upside down over smoke and fires, and hit with birch whips or canes. The victim would often be undressed, thrown from a boat into the bay and thrashed as he was trying to get back into the boat. Quite a few apprentices died as a direct cause of these games, and so they were banned in 1671. Still, in secrecy, they kept the games going for more than a century.

of houses stretching east from the front-houses on Vågen. The rows of buildings are called farms and each farm has its own name - often after its owner. From Nikolaikirkealmenning and northwards, today the farms are named the following: Holmedalsgården, Bellgården, Jakobsfjorden, Svendsgården, Enhjørningsgården, Bredsgården and Bugården.

At the top part of Bryggen, facing Øvregaten (The upper street), was an assembly building, Schøtstuene, with a dining hall, a kitchen, and gardens for herbs and vegetables.

Bryggen's original shoreline was at least a hundred metres closer to the buildings than the present quay. After each fire the farms were extended, and bit by bit, the dock basin was filled in. As a result, a large part of the buildings were built on piles. In front of the façade-buildings, which were formerly seaside warehouses with pulleys, smaller quays were set up. Big derricks were used to load and unload the vessels. The quay we have today, long and continuous, emerged in the 13th century.

This area was called Tyskebryggen (The German wharf) because, in the medieval age and especially after the Black Plague, it was inhabited and run by Hanseatic merchants. For long periods of time they dominated Bryggen; the trading activity of Bergen, shipping, import and export of Stock fish.

The Hanseatic wharf was its own community with its own set of customs

From Bryggen.

and rules. The German merchants and their employees were, for instance, prohibited to bring women from Germany and to marry women from Bergen. Thus flourished the brothels along Øvregaten. (The upper street).

Even though the Hanseatic League had many privileges, it was not free to do as it pleased. The fact that Rosenkrantz tower was built, somewhat threateningly, to face inwards towards the town, was an expression and a demonstration of royalty's desire to keep an eye on the Hanseatic office.

At the end of the 16th century, the power of the Hanseatic League weakened, but there were still boys from Bremen, Rostock, Lübeck and Stralsund arriving to work as servants at Bryggen until the 17th century.

After the Hanseatic League lost all its power, slowly but surely, Bryggen became Norwegian.

At the end of the 18th century, attempts were made to make landlords reconstruct the area. Thankfully, the attempts were only successful on half of the settlement. The main part of southern Bryggen was torn down around 1900 and replaced by brick houses. Although taller than their wooden neighbours, the stylish characteristics and pointed façades of these new buildings caused them to harmonize well.

Two of the houses furthest south at Bryggen were not included in the reconstruction. One of them, Kjøttbasaren (the meat market), was built from 1874-76, and was thus considered a new building when the modernization plans first occurred. With its Neo-Romanesque architecture, Kjøttbasaren is a good example of a Norwegian building within the Hanover-school. It went through a successful restoration and modernization a couple of years ago, and today it houses an upper-scale food market and a pharmacy.

The other building not touched by the reconstruction was Finnegaarden, the only remaining older farm south of Nikolaikirkeallmenning. The brick-extension along the southern side of the building was added in 1870, in the same architectural style as Kjøttbasaren. The Hanseatic Museum is situated in one part of Finnegården.

Bryggen is Bergen's number one pride. These days it houses handicraft shops and several cafés whose tables line the pavement. On a quiet summer evening, when sunset brushes her golden colours over the façades of Bryggen, you'll find the Bergenser moved to tears.

The meat market was the butchers' house. Today it houses stalls for food-lovers.

⊳ *A summer's day on Bryggen.*

Norwegian Museum of fisheries is placed on Bon-telabo north of the Haakon's hall and the fortress of Bergenhus. It has an extencive collection from the Norwegian history of fishing..

⟨ *Statsraad Lehmkuhl.*

THE SEAFARING TOWN

Bergen has always been a seafaring town. In the 18th century the ship owners of Bergen modernized the Norwegian merchant fleet and pioneered the transition from sails to steam. There were many shipyards, and all kinds of ships from Bergen still cross the oceans. With its surroundings, including an oil refinery 10 miles north of the city, the harbour in Bergen is one of the busiest ports in Europe.

Liner vessels are another important part of the shipping history of Bergen. There was a scheduled route from Bergen to New York running from the ferry port Skoltegrunnskaien by the fortress of Bergenhus, and many Norwegians emigrated to America from Bergen.

There are still scheduled passenger ferries operating between Bergen–Denmark, Bergen–England (Newcastle), and Bergen–Scotland/The Faeroe Islands/Iceland.

Bergen is called «The Fjord Capital», or «The Gateway to the Fjords» and is Norway's biggest cruise ship harbour.

It's also the starting point for Hurtigruten, the passenger ferry servicing the stretch of coast from Bergen up to Kirkenes, close to the Russian border. This cruise takes ten days, and it is said to be the world's most beautiful coastal voyage.

Many a proud ship has belonged to the Bergen shipyards, but if you ask people from Bergen today which they appreciate the most, they'll answer the Statsraad Lemkuhl and Beffen. Both have their own permanent spot on the quayside between Bryggen and Rosenkrantz tower, and both characterize the waterfront of Bergen. As Beffen charmingly chugs over Vågen with her passengers, the Statsraad Lehmkuhl sits majestically by the quay. The Statsraad Lemkuhl is a baroque with wooden masts which was first set afloat in 1914 as a school training ship in Bremerhaven, Germany under the name «Grossherzog Friedrich August». Few people from Bergen are familiar with this name - they call it Statsraad Lehmkuhl, after the man who acquired it and brought it to Bergen in 1923. It continued to be a school training ship until 1966. Today the ship is owned by a foundation which rents it out to

The present Bryggen and Vågen.

private and public companies. It is quite safe to say that taking a journey across the North Sea on the Statsraad Lehmkuhl would be a dream come true for the majority of Bergen's citizens.

Beffen is named after the shipping company which once owned it, «BEF» or «Bergens Elektriske Fergeselskap». Beffen is the last survivor of the many small ferries that crossed the harbour basin up until the 1960's. It has a steady schedule every working day of the week, and it serves as Bergen's mascot.

UNDER DANISH AND SWEDISH RULE

When the Norwegian king Haakon Magnusson died in 1380 the country faced a new situation. The king was married to the daughter of the Danish king, Margrete, and the son of Haakon and Margrete, Olav, was elected king of Denmark in 1375. When his father died Olav became king of Norway as well. Thus, the two countries joined in a union that would last until 1814. The Danish aristocracy, bureaucracy and language dominated the union.

Bergen's status in the Late Middle Ages was weak. Shipping was at an all-time low, but things would turn around in the 15th century. Two Danish feudal overlords, Kristoffer Valkendorf and Erik Rosenkrantz, challenged the power of the Hanseatic League. The new neighbourhoods that had emerged along the south and west sides of Vågen were reserved for the town's new middle classes. Immigration strengthened the bourgeoisie. For instance, the Dutch made a great impact on the town's shipping industry. At the end of the 15th century, merchant vessels from Bergen sailed from Arkangelsk in the north to Sicily in the south. The goods they exported remained more or less the same throughout history: Stock fish, cod liver oil, roe, salted fish, and sometimes klippfisk and timber.

Denmark-Norway sided with the French during the Napoleonic Wars. The Swedes however fought with the winning team, so Denmark had to part with Norway in 1814 as war trade to Sweden. But Norway wasn't about to be pushed around without a fight. The idea of independence had long been considered. Throughout Norway representatives were being elected to form a national assembly at Eidsvoll, where they would pass the Norwegian constitution on the 17th of May. Several men from Bergen took a central part at Eidsvoll, all fronting a free Norway. The idea of independence was nonetheless abandoned, and the union with Sweden lasted from 1814 until 1905, but the constitution still existed.

When Norway finally declared itself free and independent on the 7th of June, 1905, it was led by Christian Michelsen, the shipowner and politician from Bergen. He became the first prime minister of an independent Norway.

Michelsen's residence, Gamlehaugen (the old hill), was completed in the year 1900. He lived there until he died in 1925. Gamlehaugen was designed by the architect J.Z.M. Kielland. Today it belongs to the royal family and the state of Norway. In the surrounding gardens, open to the public year-round, you'll find an abundance of rhododendrons. There are guided tours through parts of the building during the tourist season.

Slaget paa Bergens Vaag 1665. Efter en samtidig Tegning.

THE BATTLE OF VÅGEN

In 1664 war broke out between England and Holland. In the summer of 1665, Dutch ships returning from the East Indies gathered in neutral Bergen harbour for shelter with cargos of millions of guilders in value. The king of Denmark-Norway knew this, and made a secret deal with the king of England letting the English conquer the Dutch fleet. Later the loot was to be divided equally between the two kingdoms. In August the English with their 14 frigates, four galleys and three fireships sailed towards Bergen. The military leaders at the fortress of Bergenshus, having not yet received the order from the king to aid the English, thus chose to support the attacked party. There was a stupendous battle. The English fleet had close to 1,000 cannons, the Dutch a bit fewer. From the fortress in Bergen, 10 small bronze cannons and 100 iron cannons were used. In the end, the English retreated with 6-700 wounded or dead. The Dutch lost considerably fewer. Ten civilians also lost their lives and the English cannonballs greatly damaged buildings in town. One is still wedged in the tower above the entrance to the Cathedral.

⊰ *Gamlehaugen, the residence of prime minister Christian Michelsen.*

BUILDINGS AND MUSEUMS

Sverresborg fortress stands tall between the fortress of Bergenshus and Skute-viken, a town quarter with beautiful old wooden houses. It was built by King Sverre Sigurdsson in 1185. Many consider him one of the most important rulers in Norwegian history. He fled his opponents in 1198 and the fortress was destroyed. It was rebuilt, however, and King Sverre died in Bergen in 1202. He was one of the many kings to be buried in the town's first cathedral, Kristkirken, the Church of Christ. It's positioned at Holmen, where today there is a statue of saint Sunniva, the patron saint of Bergen. In 1531 Kristkirken was torn down by the Danish feudal overlord Eske Bilde and the mortal remains of the kings were lost. Eske Bilde did Bergen no good, and was also responsible for the destruction of Apostelkirken (the church of the Apostles). Sverresborg is open to visitors.

In addition to Sverresborg and Bergenshus, there was a third fortress by the harbour of Bergen; Fredriksberg. It was built after the battle of Vågen when it was decided that there should also be a fortress on the west side of the harbour basin. Fredriksberg was never used in war and served many years as a fire station. Today one of Bergen's many boys' drill corpses, Nordnes Bataljon, rehearse there.

Sverresborg.

⬯ The view from Bergenhus. In front and to the right, the twin towers of the church of St. Mary. To the left: The fire station on Skansen. Ulriken mountain in the background.

Haakon's hall and the tower of Rosenkrantz.

HAAKON'S HALL

Haakon IV Haakonsson was king of Norway from 1217 to 1263. In 1247 Haakon finally achieved recognition by the pope, who sent cardinal William of Sabina to Bergen to crown him. At that time there were two halls on Holmen. Both were too small for the coronation party, so it was held in a large boathouse. It was rainy in Bergen, then as well as now, and during the party it was raining cats and dogs. The roof was leaking, and the need for a proper hall of stone with a paved courtyard became evident. In the same year the king started the building of Haakon's Hall, which was completed in 1260.

The hall was built in granite with decorations made out of steatite. Haakon Haakonson was well acquainted with King Henry III of England and the hall is inspired by similar English and Scottish constructions.

In the Middle Ages several ceremonies were held at Haakon's Hall. Magnus Lagabøter, the son of Haakon Haakonson, married the Danish princess Ingeborg there in 1261. In due course Eirik, the son of Magnus, married the Scottish princess Margrete, daughter of King Alexander III, in the same hall.

In the 16th century Haakon's Hall was abandoned and decayed, its greatness forgotten. It was used as a granary. The great Norwegian national romantic painter I.C.Dahl (1788–1857) saw the hall as a hidden treasure and initiated restoration.

In 1944, during the Second World War, a fully loaded German ammunition ship exploded near Holmen, causing great damage to the nearby buildings, including Haakon's Hall. The restoration was resumed after the war and was completed in 1961. The roof looks the same as it did in the earliest picture of Bergen, the so called «Scholeusstikket» from 1580. The pictorial artist Sigrun Berg made the big woven piece («the primstaff») hanging on the east wall inside the hall. A primstaff is an old calendar stick marking memorable days.

Nowadays there are concerts held there during the annual Bergen International Festival, and the Holberg prize is handed out in the Hall every 3rd of December.

THE STORY OF THE SCOTSWIFE

Anna Rustung, or «the scotswife» as she was later called, was the daughter of a Norwegian admiral and nobleman. As a young woman she met the Scottish earl of Bothwell in Copenhagen. She fell in love and they became engaged. A wedding was planned and Anna Rustung brought with her a large dowry when the couple travelled together to Holland. From there the earl ran away with all of the dowry, went home to Scotland and married another woman.

In Scotland he gradually got into trouble. He was accused of taking part in the murder of Maria Stuart's husband, and the fact that he annulled his own marriage and married Maria Stuart shortly afterward did not lessen the suspicion. His enemies grew in number, and he decided to flee to Denmark/ Norway. When he got to Karmøy, south of Bergen, his ship was seized by a Norwegian/Danish battleship. He revealed his identity, but wasn't believed. He was then escorted to Bergen and given temporary residence at Rosenkrantz tower under the feudal overlord Erik Rosenkrantz while his case was investigated.

This is when he faced his nemesis. Anna Rustung had heard news of where Bothwell stayed. Through her powerful friends, she had him charged with theft of her dowry and breach of the engagement. The case against him grew large and extensive, the murder charges and flight from Scotland were implicated, and in the end the earl was convicted. He was brought from Bergen to Denmark where he went insane and ended his days locked up at the castle of Dragsholm.

Anna Rustung got her revenge, but she remained unhappy. Many people say that she haunts Rosenkrantz tower, where she last saw the earl of Bothwell. At night her ghost strolls restlessly about, and she's been spotted several times in one of the windows.

ROSENKRANTZ TOWER

A few metres south of Haakon's Hall, Rozenkrantz tower stands tall. It is a Renaissance building named after Erik Rosenkrantz, a feudal overlord at Bergenshus from 1560 to 1568. It faces the harbour and Bryggen; made to give the impression that the kingdom was watching the Hansa men.

The tower was built in 1562 over the ruins of several preceding towers from the Middle Ages, when the fortress of Bergenshus was at its peak in size. At that time the tower was a part of the royal residency as well as a fortress.

The tower of Rosenkrantz.

Throughout the years Rosenkrantz tower has changed a great deal. A lot of these changes were made after the explosion at Bryggen in 1944, when a large part of it was ruined. Before the restoration was initiated, it was decided that the structures from the different epochs would be preserved. Consequently, some of the floors have two levels. A part of the house chapel from the era of King Magnus the Lawmender was preserved, as well as a dungeon in the basement that was used as a prison from the 17th century until 1870.

CHURCH OF THE CROSS

The Church of the Cross is dedicated to the Holy Cross. The church was originally a long church with wooden towers, oriented east-west, constructed in a Romanesque style preceding 1181. The stone tower was not built until 1594. The wings of the church were built in the 16th century. From the picture «Scholeusstikket» it is apparent that the church once had a twin tower, similar to St. Mary's Church.

The Church of the Cross was a church for royalty and the garrison. On June 18th, 1858 the author Henrik Ibsen married Susanne Daae Thoresen here. Her father was the pastor of the church at the time.

Today the Church of the Cross is open to anyone's needs. The Bergen mission works from here, and the church has its own street vicar.

Outside the church a memorial made out of canons and anchor chains stands to commemorate the fallen in the battle of Alvøen in 1808.

ST. MARY'S CHURCH

The oldest building still existing in Bergen in its original form. It's very distinctive with its twin towers. Its construction was probably started back in the 10th century, but was not finished until 1184. Its architectural style is prima-

THE BATTLE OF ALVØEN – DAVID VS. GOLIATH

During the Napoleonic Wars, Norway/Denmark sided with Napoleon. Bergen was shielded against hostile attacks, but the English blocked the Norwegian coast. Essential foods did not reach the town and the people from Bergen suffered as a result. In 1808 the English frigate «Tartar» sailed towards the shore south of Bergen under false flags and with alarming intentions. After some adversities however the captain decided to sail back out to sea. All sails were raised, but there was no wind, and outside Alvøen the Norwegian gunboat flotilla, one barge and four jollies caught up with the English frigate. The small boats opened fire. Under normal circumstances the Norwegian flotilla would stand no chance against their powerful enemy, but the lack of wind made manoeuvring difficult for the frigate. The men from Bergen made good use of the fact that they knew the waters well. The first shot they fired killed the captain and the «Tartar» was seriously damaged. The frigate was about to strike their flag when it got windy and they managed to escape. The incident was named «The battle of Alvøen» and helped raise the spirits of the people from Bergen in otherwise bleak times.

The church of St. Mary.

rily Romanesque with high Gothic elements. Amongst the church's treasures is a triptych made in Lübeck in the late 14th century, and a pulpit made in Norway in 1677 in Baroque style. Shaped by the woodcarver Søren Olsen, the apostles in the choir date back to 1632. Other decorative art worth mentioning are the epitaphs, the oldest one from 1585, together with some Rubens copies painted by Elias Figenschou in 1650.

The church was used by the Hanseatic league and was called «the German church» by locals.

St. Mary's Church is in use today as a parish church, and as its acoustics are very good, it's often used for concerts.

THE CATHEDRAL

The Cathedral was originally named St. Olav's Church. The church was devoted to the Norwegian saint Olav, and was conveyed to the Franciscan order. After the Danish feudal overlord Eske Bilde tore down the original Cathedral from the Middle Ages, church of Christ, St. Olav's Church became the Cathedral of Bergen.

The Cathedral played an important part in the period after the Reformation and was linked to education through its closest neighbour, the Latin School, Schola Bergensis or «Bergen Katedralskole» as it was later to be named. The Latin School's old building and the new school are situated on

The cathedral.

either side of the church. The school was founded by the cardinal Nicholas Breakspear – later pope Adrian IV – in 1153.

In the small cemetery on the northern side of the church the composer of the song of Bergen, bishop Johan Nordahl Brun, is buried.

TWO WOODEN CHURCHES, FANTOFT AND ST. JØRGEN

The Norwegian stave churches are the eldest preserved wooden churches, with a unique architecture. They date back as far as the 11th century. Between 1000 and 2000 of these kinds of churches were built in Norway. 28 still exist today, one of them being Fantoft stave church (Fantoft stavkirke) right outside of Bergen. It was originally built near the eastern end of Sognefjord around the year 1150. It was moved to Bergen in 1883. In 1992 the church was totally destroyed by arson. Reconstruction of the church was promptly initiated. The existing church is an exact copy.

St. Jørgen is a small simple church with a very special history. It was originally built in the 14th century as a church for people in town struck with leprosy. It burned down twice, in 1640 and 1702, and the existing building dates back to 1703. St. Jørgen's Hospital, or the Leprosy Museum, is the church's neighbour. The museum shows the illness' history in Norway and depicts life in the hospital. The Norwegian doctor Armauer Hansen's discovery of the Lepra germ greatly impacted work with lepers worldwide. The Lepra archives in Bergen are included in the Memory of the World International Register of UNESCO.

St. Jørgen hospital and church is a peaceful oasis in the midst of town.

⪡ Fantoft stave church.

BERGEN MUSEUM

Wilhelm Fredrik Koren Christie played a leading role during the consti-
tutional gathering at Eidsvoll in 1814, and later he became a member of
parliament. However, his heart's innermost desire was to have a museum in
Bergen. In 1825, Christie founded Bergen Museum.

Since its existence was built on seafare and foreign trade, there were,
needless to say, many widely-travelled people in Bergen. A vast amount of
strange articles were hence brought to Bergen from overseas. Due to his wide

The natural history collection. The president of the Storting is guarding the whale skeletons ...

variety of contacts, and to the fact that he was a collector by nature, Christie was able to obtain these and other such articles.

A statue of the founder stands in front of the beautiful building at Sydneshaugen, designed by architect Johan Henrik Nebelong, where the collection moved to in 1865. A large section of The University of Bergen is situated at Sydneshaugen and today the collection is in two buildings.

Consisting mainly of the zoology and geology fields, The Natural History collection can be found in the Nebelong museum building from 1865. Parts of the collection have been updated and modernised, whilst other parts have been kept the same since the 19th century - making the collection itself emerge as a museum of a museum. In the whale hall, where unique whale skeletons and stuffed sea-creatures reside, you will find one of the most magnificent collections. Plenty of strange items are also on display in the museum, for example a piece of a boat penetrated by a sword-fish!

A building previously known as the History Museum, is now the home of the Cultural History collection. It was designed by the architect Egill Reimers, and was put to use for this purpose in 1927. Amongst other interesting objects from Bergen Museum's early days, this building still holds a collection of Egyptian mummies. In the ethnographic collection, along with displays originating from ethnic communities all over the world, objects from Polonesia and Oceania are found. As well as artistic church and ancient peasant objects, the museum proudly displays remnants from a range of styles taken from different eras of Bergen's city culture. The Cultural History collection also holds the Theatre collection, established by the former Bergen Theatre Museum, with amongst other things, a model of the old theatre which was ruined by bombs in 1944. A number of articles from the time Henrik Ibsen lived, can also be found here.

BRYGGEN MUSEUM

In 1955 Bryggen caught fire, hopefully for the last time. Initiated by the archaeologist Asbjørn Herteig, archaeological diggings were started at the fire site, and the everyday life of the average citizen in the Middle Ages came to light.

Along with fish traps containing remains of fish, mooring equipment, other tools and sanitary articles; carved inscriptions were also discovered.

The architect for Bryggens Museum, which was built in 1976 on the outskirts of this site, was Øyvind Maurseth. As an attempt to show how the people of Bryggen lived around the year 1300, findings from the archaeological diggings are on display in the museum. Parts of a huge cargo ship used as building elements in the old houses, are also on display.

THE HANSEATIC MUSEUM

The Hanseatic Museum in Finnegården at Bryggen was founded in 1872. It shows an original interior from the time of German office, and emits a living impression of what it must have looked like in the backyards of Bryggen at the time of Hanseatic dominance. The items in the museum come

Finnegården with the Fløien mountain in the background.

THE RUNES

The Runes are a set of Germanic symbols which were used prior to the latin alphabet. Inscription of runes could be found on weapons, tools and jewellery – or as messages or proverbs on small flat sticks. The carvings on one of them very clearly states that the local pub could stop a man from performing his matrimonial duties. The inscription says: «Gyda tells you to go home». A stick could also be carved in verses.

Such were found during the archaeological diggings on Bryggen in 1955, and brought new knowledge on early Norwegian poetry. In Norway you'll also find runes on memorial stones. The oldest inscriptions dates back to 200 AD.

from these old backyards, enabling us to see how people worked and lived. «Schøttstuene», situated by the Maria Church, is also a part of this museum.

OLD BERGEN

Old Bergen is an open-air museum situated a couple of kilometres north of the city centre. Due to the development of modern town planning leading to the demolition of houses and blocks, several old buildings were moved to Old Bergen. The museum aims to give an impression of how the city functioned between the years 1700–1800. The interiors of several houses show shops and workshops as they once were. Among other things, you will find the workshop of a baker, a dentist and a photographer. The museum also has a large collection of portraits – some of which can be found on the internet.

Old Bergen arranges different activity days and has its own travelling theatre which cooperates with Vestlandske Teatersenter.

Old Bergen.

THE ART MUSEUMS

The architect Henry Bucher designed Vestlandske Kunstindustrimuseum, a monumental building from 1896 at «Permanenten». The museum is beautifully situated by the city park, and on its front is a sculpture of the painter I.C. Dahl, carved by Ambrosia Tønnesen.

The collections in the museum include old silverware, ornaments and textiles. The museum also contains a large and valuable collection left by the Bergenser and general J.W. Munthe. He led a manifold and peculiar life and at the beginning of the 20th century, sent many objects from China to Bergen. Unique amongst the museum's items is Ole Bull's Gasparo da Saldo violin from 1562.

The Lille Lungegårdsvann with Lysverket in the background.

Four buildings containing art galleries can be found just across the road by Lille Lungegårdsvann. Three of these buildings constitute Bergens Kunstmuseum and hold permanent art exhibitions. In May, the Japanese cherry trees bloom around Lille Lungegårdsvann, followed by roses and rhododendrons. This colourful flora makes the surrounding area an attraction in itself. These four buildings give a varied but harmonious impression of the almost one hundred years of architecture for this kind of building.

The Stenersamlingen was given to Bergen as a gift by the art patron Rolf Stenersen, and the architect was Sverre Lied. Originally, the collection consisted of contemporary art and artwork from the 20th century. Since 2003, a

vast amount of the paintings from the Stenersamlingen were moved to Lysverket and the exhibitions shown at Stenersamlingen now are mainly temporary.

Rasmus Meyers samlinger was also a testimonial gift given to (the council of) Bergen in 1924 by the heirs of the art collector Rasmus Meyer. The building was drawn by architect Ole Landmark, and it was constructed in 1924. The collection here includes important works of art from Norwegian artists, such as significant paintings by I.C. Dahl, and a collection of the works of Edvard Munch. The Rasmus Meyers collection also has historical pieces of furniture and interiors taken and preserved from old houses in Bergen. One of the special attractions is the rococo-room, decorated by the painter Mathias Blumenthal (1719–1763).

Lysverket is a functionalistic building from 1939 designed by the architects Fredrik Arnesen and Arthur Darre Kaarbø. As the Norwegian meaning of its name depicts, this building previously housed the administration of the Bergen Electricity (Lysverker) company. Today the building exhibits a composition of historical works by Norwegian and foreign artists. Much attention and space has been dedicated to I.C. Dahl and his students, and Norwegian contemporary art is also considerably represented.

Between Stenersamlingen and Rasmus Meyers Samlinger, we find Bergen Kunsthall which continuously shows new exhibitions of works by Norwegian and foreign contemporary artists. In this building we also find a cafe and Landmark bar - meeting places for the new and experimental generations.

BERGEN
CULTURE CITY

The arts have always held a steadfast position between the seven mountains of Bergen. The runes from Bryggen are fine examples of some of the oldest writings in Scandinavian history. Due to the fact that several languages were spoken in the Middle Ages, foreign works were translated to Norwegian at many desks in Bergen.

Formed as a conversation between father and son, the most magnificent Norwegian work from the early Middle Ages «Kongespeilet», was written in Bergen between 1196 and 1260. The son asks questions and the father answers, giving advice about different matters, including how to conduct oneself courteously abroad.

Several renowned authors grew up in Bergen in the 16th century. They recorded the events of their time and were educated humanitarians who were true to the contemporary style of their art.

The 17th century saw the breakthrough of pure, fictional prose. Dorothe Engelbrechtdatter (1634–1716) was the first Norwegian female who was able to live off her writing.

The foremost native figure in literature, perhaps of all time, is considered to be the author of comedy, Ludvig Holberg (1684–1759). He grew up during the time Bergen bore evidence of immigration from the whole of Northern Europe, and with great exuberance he wrote «Bergens Beskrivelse» (a description of Bergen) - a depiction of street life in his childhood city. Holberg was a pupil at Bergen Katedralskole. He became familiar with theater as an actor in the school's traditional drama productions. Even though Holberg emigrated to Copenhagen at the age of 20 and was never to return, his comedies have been performed innumerable times on the stages of Bergen. Along with historic and philosophic works, Holberg wrote the novel «Niels Klims Travels to The Underworld». In this story the main character falls down a familiar hole in Bergen, the «Mareminehollet» and ends up in the underworld. The novel mocks human foolishness and criticises the society of those days.

From the festival town Bergen a sunny day in May.

The statue of Amalie Skram on Klosteret.

By endorsement of the State Norway, The Holberg Prize and The Niels Klims Prize are annually handed out on December the 3rd, the writer's birthday. A statue of Holberg stands at Vågsallmenning, by Torget.

Amalie Skram (1846–1905) is another great author from Bergen. Her fervent four volumed family-cycle novel «Hellemyrsfolket» portrays a strong naturalistic picture of the dark side of Bergen in the 19th century. A statue of Amalie Skram stands in a part of town called Klosteret at Nordnes.

Nordahl Grieg (1902–1943) was a journalist, an author and a citizen committed to the good of society. He wrote politically provocative poems, plays and novels. As a journalist and editor of contemporary writing in the 1930s,

he warned against Nazism. When war broke out in Norway on April the 9th, 1940, he threw himself into the cause to fight for his country. From then on his works brought the nation together. After joining the Norwegian forces in England, Greig became an officer and a war correspondent. Simultaneously, he wrote patriotic poems which were sent by air waves from London to the many Norwegians risking their lives by gathering around illegal radios. As a war correspondent, Greig participated in several flight exploits, and he was shot down and killed over Berlin in 1943. The Nordahl Greig statue stands by «Den Nationale Scene» (The National Theatre).

Nordahl Grieg.

The early writings of Torbjørg Nedraas (1906–1900) were also influenced by the war and the years of occupation. From a number of her books, the portrayals of female characters have been entrenched in Norwegian literature. Close to a part of town called Møhlenpris, not far from where the author grew up, we find Torbjørg Nedraas Street.

The first play known to be performed in Bergen was «Adam's Fall». This event took place in front of Domkirken in 1562 and its initiator was the humanist, historian, author and headmaster of Bergen Katedralskole, Absalon Pederssøn Beyer (1528–1575). In the 17th century, classic tragedies and morality plays were performed by the pupils, including Ludvig Holberg, as previously mentioned.

Towards the end of the 18th century, several drama companies were established in Norway. One such company was set up in Bergen in 1794. Six years later, the Komediehuset (House of Comedy) at Engen came into use, and its opening performance took place on Holberg's birthday. Founded by Ole Bull in 1850, The Norwegian Theatre was housed in the same building as Komediehuset, which was Northern Europe's oldest civilian theatrical building. The theatre was of great significance to the development of Norwegian as a stage language.

Ole Bull recognised the talent of the young Henrik Ibsen as a dramatist and in 1851 he employed him as dramatical writer and scene instructor. Ibsen lived in Bergen from the age of 23 to 29, from the period of 1851 to 1857. Another celebrated Norwegian author, Bjørnstjerne Bjørnson, was the artistic director for two years.

Following bankruptcy in 1863, The Norwegian Theatre was revived thirteen years later as «The National Scene» in the same building. Einar O. Schou was the architect of The National Venue of Theatre's «new building», which was an awarded Jugend building completed in 1909. This beautiful

⊳ *Vågsalmenningen with the statue of Holberg in the centre.*

The statue of Ibsen stands by Den Nationale Scene, Bergen's theatre.

building was ruined by bomb attacks in the Second World War.

The legendary violinist and composer Ole Bull was born in Bergen in 1810. On his tours around the world, he was a worshipped idol playing for emperors and kings. Ole Bull was influenced by contemporary national romantic idealism, and two buildings in Bergen and the surrounding area bear his name. One of these buildings lies north of Bergen at Osterøy. The other,

a fantastic wooden house he had built as his country home, is a kind of Swiss villa with an onion shaped dome in Mauritian style. This imaginative house is situated south of Bergen at Lysøen and now serves as a museum. Ole Bull died in Bergen in 1880 and in his own peculiar spirit, one could say, a large urn containing the composer's earthly ashes has been placed on the pedestal of the assistant churchyard by Stadsporten close to the city centre. A sculpture of Ole Bull and his mythological source of inspiration, «Nøkken»

Ole Bull was in his days worshipped as rockstars are worshipped today.

⊃ Edvard and Nina Grieg.

(a waterfall creature with a violin), stands at Ole Bull's plass in the centre of Bergen.

Ole Bull discovered the young Edvard Grieg (born in 1843) and made provisions for his music education in Leipzig. Grieg spent much of his time in Hardanger and was inspired by Norwegian folk music. The Edvard Grieg statue stands in the city park, near Lille Lungegaardsvann.

From the 20th century we can mention composers such as Harald Sæverud. He used music actively in the struggle against the Nazi occupation of Norway in the Second World War. In support of the Norwegian resistance, he wrote «Kjempeviseslåtten», among other things.

TROLDHAUGEN

After many years of travelling overseas, the world famous composer Grieg and his wife Nina returned to Bergen and had their house designed by the architect Schak Bull.

Troldhaugen at Hop, just under 10 kilometres from the centre of Bergen, was where Greig and his wife Nina settled. Their furniture, including Grieg's Steinway grand piano from 1892, has been preserved.

Edvard and Nina were very hospitable, and many contemporary artists and personalities visited the couple at Troldhaugen. Whenever it got too crowded, Grieg found refuge in the little hut he composed in, situated on a peaceful spot away from the main house. In the hut were his piano, desk and chaise longue.

USF.

THE CULTURE CITY OF TODAY

Today, Bergen's culture blossoms and is more multi-facetted than ever before. The city is the home of countless musicians, authors, artists, dancers, etc. Many of these make use of USF (United Sardine Factory) – which was once the city's largest sardine factory. Here we find offices for artist groups and art organisations; workshops for craftsmen, designers, artists and film producers; as well as exhibition rooms, theatre and concert halls and a hall for the film club.

Bergen has art schools and art colleges, music schools and a writing academy. Established art institutes and new experimental groups co-exist, and many stages are available for theatre productions and concerts. The largest of these stages are housed by The National Venue of Theatre and the concert hall Greighallen – the main headquarters for the Bergen Philharmonic Orchestra. Moreover, Bergen today is the centre for music in all forms. As well as corps and its traditions, rock music has long since come to stay on the stages of Bergen.

Experimental and new groups are represented by the Bergen International Theatre which presents leading avant-garde groups from home and abroad. Carte Blanche,

Norway's national dance company also serves this purpose. Among others, Carte Blanche co-operates with BIT20, the city's permanent orchestra for contemporary music.

Permanent and sporadic festivals flourish in Bergen. In the summer there's the Eggstock rock festival, and in the autumn the Bergen International Film Festival shows films from all over the world. In November there's the «Forfattersleppet» which is when new books are released for sale.

Most festivals start in the spring, bringing vitality and nourishment to the mentality of the citizens of Bergen, a much appreciated blessing after a long and wet winter.

The first festival of the year is Bergenfest at the end of April with blues and country music etc., played by Norwegian and foreign artists. Followed by this is

Grieghallen.

Carte Blanche - The Norwegian National Company of Contemporary Dance.

the Nattjazzen at the end of May. Nattjazzen is a part of the great Festspillene i Bergen, which was originally a festival for classical music, but is now open to all of the arts. Crowds from home and abroad stream to these festivals, sometimes making it a struggle to get ahold of tickets.

As the spring festivals in Bergen burst with joy, music can be heard from small and large concert halls in all corners of the city. Sounds of voices and laughter seep from restaurants and bars, and out in the streets and open spaces, musicians, jugglers and theatre groups conjure up performances to suit all tastes. If you happen to be there then, when the sun shines at the end of May, you will be greeted by Bergen at its best.

HANDICRAFT AND DESIGN

Craftsmen and designers display their goods in shops around town. Among other places, local fashion designers have shops in Stølegaten, Steinkjellergaten and Skostredet (The Shoe Alley). As the name suggests, Skostredet used to house over 40 shoemakers. Today the street is known for its vinyl record stores and youthful atmosphere. Antiques and rarities can be found in Øvregaten, Lille Øvregaten, Øvre Korskirkealmenningen and Kong Oscars gate.

↪ *Vestlandske Kunstindustrimuseum.*

UP FLØIEN AND
BACK DOWN

Bergen is situated between seven mountains. People from Bergen do not agree as to which mountains are actually included in this number. There is an ongoing discussion regarding whether Storavarden or Askefjellet should be counted as part of the Bergen mountains, as they are located at Askøy, outside Bergen's borders. Some Bergensers have a hard time including them.

Two of the mountains everybody agrees should be counted are Fløien (325 meters above sea level) and Ulriken (643 meters above sea level). Both have funiculars that carry people to the top and lovely views of Bergen and its surroundings. The oldest and most famous is the funicular of Fløien. It's an electrical cable railway with an 850 metre-long track. At its steepest it slopes 26 degrees. Like Statsraad Lehmkul and Beffen, it's one of the mascots of Bergen. The funicular terminal station is on Vetrlidsalmenning, east of the fish market, and its final stop is on the top of Fløien. There you'll find a restaurant which is open in the summer. The funicular usually departs every half hour. It's a means of transportation for the people living on the mountainside, and stops at the top of Promsgate, on Fjellveien and Skansemyren. During the tourist season it has continuous departures.

The funicular of Fløien was opened in 1918. The wagons were replaced in 1954 and 2000, when the rails also were replaced. Next to its terminal station you'll find a bust of Waldemar Stoud Platou, the funicular's initiator. One of the people who fought to build it was the Prime Minister Christian Michelsen.

THE VIEW FROM FLØIEN

Come along to the funicular of Fløien, pay your fair and follow us to the top of the mountain. Once there, we can enjoy the view of Bergen and its fjord.

On your right hand side you can see Bryggen, Sverresborg and the fortress of Bergenshus with Haakon's hall and Rosenkrants tower. Skoltegrunnskaien lies there with its cruise ships and North Sea ferries. We might also see other vessels in the harbour and on the city's fjord; cargo ships, trawlers, supply boats

and pleasure boats. Express boats leaving for and coming from places along the coast of Norway are going in both northern and southern directions.

On the western side of Vågen (the bay) the city stretches an arm towards the north, culminating in Nordnes park and the aquarium. Most buildings on the beach side of the Nordnes peninsula are new. Fires, war and city planners lacking an aesthetic sense removed hundreds of the original wooden buildings.

THE TV-TOWER ON ULRIKEN

The people of Bergen love their city and react very strongly to any talk of change. Here's a good example: In 1961 TV had already existed in Oslo for a couple of years, and so it was Bergen's turn. The decision to build a TV-tower on Ulriken, visible from the whole town, was protested loudly by the people of Bergen. Angry letters were sent to editors and a petition was started. Today this has all been forgotten. At night the tower on Ulriken is beautified with multicoloured lights.

Just below us lies the small Lungegaards Lake lined by art museums with Grieg hall right behind it. You can also make out Bergen museum consisting of two big yellow buildings on the upper right.

Further south of the little Lungegaards Lake lies the big Lungegaards Lake. Once upon a time these were connected by a narrow neck of water. The big Lungegaards Lake is the actual end of the fjord. The water level has sunk with time. Buildings and roads bearing uneven levels of aesthetic quality have risen where the water used to be. This big road spaghetti connects the main roads entering from the southwest and north. Further south the valley of Bergen stretches towards new and densely populated suburbs.

West of town lie three of seven mountains in a row. From south to north you can make out Løvstakken, Damsgaardsfjellet and Lyderhorn. Along the fjord by the foot of these mountains lie factories side by side, and at the head of the fjord lie the biggest shipyards. Bergen was not just a trading and shipping town, it was also an industrial city. Today just one of the shipbuilding yards remains. It's situated in Laksevåg, the part of town that lies just across the fjord from the Nordnes peninsula. We can see it clearly from Fløien.

Behind the three mountains lie new suburbs. Bergen has grown both in population and size. Most people from Bergen don't live in the city centre but behind the seven mountains.

⋙ *Bergen cable car opened in* 1961. *From here you've got a splendid view over the town, the islands west of town, the western archipelago and the ocean.*

Torgallmenningen, the rallying point of town.

ALONG THE AXIS OF TOWN

Let's take the funicular down and stroll amongst the swarms of people in town.

From the funicular we wander down to the Torget, the market square also known as the fish market. Furthest down on the market square lies Kjøttba-saren on our right. On our left hand side we see Kong Oscars gate (street). For centuries it used to be the main approach into town for trading peasants from the south.

We wait for the green man, then cross the street to the market. All year round there is seafood, fruit and vegetables for sale. Market stalls containing jewellery, gaudy finery and Norwegian knitwear pop up in the summer season. Some are authentic arts and crafts articles while others are not.

Right opposite Vågsalmenningen the author Ludvig Holberg stands tall on his pedestal watching the crowd. The big building housing the tourist information used to be the town's stock market. Frantz Willhelm Schiertz

THE AQUARIUM

The Aquarium at Nordnes was opened in 1960, but later went through several renovations. Through big panes of glass in the circular hall you can observe fish and other creatures from the Norwegian waters. The aquarium also displays a large range of salt and freshwater fish from all over the world.

was the architect and inside the building the painter Axel Revold has made a fresco.

From Torget we toddle off to the seafaring monument on Torgallmenningen. This is the main square of the city centre, where elderly ladies of Bergen sit on benches with pale faces turned towards the sun. Some people actually claim that in Bergen there are just two seasons; the gray and the green.

Most buildings around the square were raised after the fire in 1916 and designed by the architect Finn Berger. In the southeast corner lies Sundt, a functionalistic building from 1938 drawn by Per Grieg. Torgallmenningen is also called the big public sitting room of Bergen. A loud public discussion took place before a major restoration in 2000. Everyone, as mentioned earlier, is a specialist on their hometown. A group of artists, architects and designers are responsible for the new design of Torgallmenningen. Bård Breivik, an internationally known sculptor, designed the new pillars.

Torgallmenningen ends where Ole Bulls square begins. Several of Bergen's theatres are situated in this square. There is also a big block of granite named «the blue stone», a regular meeting point for Bergen's youth, especially when they celebrate on Friday and Saturday evenings.

If we want, we could continue straight ahead through western Torgate, and pass the supporter pub of our local football team. From there we'll go up the stairs to the church of Johannes. This is the biggest church in town, consecrated in 1894. Before we enter to have a closer look we'll turn around and enjoy the splendid view.

The church of John.

༊༊ *Nordnes.*

TWO SHORT
WALKS

FIRST WALK

We start at Torgallmenningen and follow Markeveien north. Where the roads levels off we spot a yellow ochre brick house with turrets. It is called «corps de garde» and from the 17th century it was used as the headquarters for fire-watchers and civic guards patrolling the streets. On the opposite side of Markeveien we descend the most famous street in Bergen, the steep Knausesmuget. If you were raised here you would be regarded as a kind of super-bergenser. Notice the middle part of the cobblestone street. The inclined line of stones in the middle were made for horses hooves and as brakes for wagoners. There are still many steep streets with these kinds of cobblestones in Bergen.

We walk down Skottegaten «The street of Scots» and turn right. This was the centre of a neighbourhood characterized by Scottish craftsmen and sailors who settled in Bergen in the 16th century. We pass blocks of flats and old wooden houses. We follow this street further on to Nedre Strangehagen and Verftsbakken, then we go down to the long quay by the fjord. It lies in front of USF (United Sardines Factory) formerly a fish factory, now housing artists. If it is spring or summer, and hot, we can sit down and drink a coffee, or have a glass of something nice, and enjoy life.

On our way back we turn up and to our left, following Verftsbakken and Strangehagen to the Convent. On a slope in front of a little park there is a statue of Amalie Skram. The house where she lived is in Cort Piils Smug (alley) to the left of Corps de Garde. A plaque is attached to the wall. We follow Cort Piils Smug a few meters down, turn to the right and go through lille (little) Markeveien, also a part of old Bergen. There we enter Østre (eastern) Muralmenning and go down to Muren (The Wall) where there's been a shop since the 16th century. We cross the street to Strandkaien and follow Vågen (the bay) back to Torgallmenningen.

In the alleyways.

Get your fresh fish here!

SECOND WALK

We start from Torget (the market) and walk upwards between Kjøttbasaren and Finnegården until we arrive at Øvregaten. During the first centuries of the town's existence churches lay side by side in this street. There were also many workshops for craftsmen here. After the Hanseatic League invaded, the space between the bars and brothels grew smaller, even less than there had been between the churches. At the start of the 15th century there were 29 houses in Øvregaten containing «women of easy virtue».

We follow Øvregaten two blocks to the north and turn towards Nicolaikirkeallmenningen, named after one of the many long gone churches. At the top of the square, we enter Steinkjellergaten to the left. From there we follow the street signs and walk up Steinkjellerbakken, Søndre Steinkjellersmuget, Nedre Blekevei and Telthussmauget to Øvre Blekevei. We are standing in one of the typical old neighbourhoods of town. Drumming buekorps boys announce the spring every single year amongst these white wooden houses.

At the end of the street we find ourselves in front of the old fire station of Skansen, built in 1903. From the tower, firemen guarded the city day and night with Argus eyes. Before we go down to Torget (you can't miss it) we have another look at town. It is still the most beautiful city in Norway.

Welcome to Bergen. Enjoy your stay – and pray to the gods for nice weather!

LITERATURE:

Berg, Adolph 1925. Bergen i gamle dage. Oslo.Bergen bys historie, Bd. I–IV. Bergen 1993–1995.

Blanc, T. 1884. Norges første nationale scene. Kristiania.

Brosing, Gustav 1955. Det gamle Bergen. Bergen.

Dagsland, Sissel Hamre (mfl.) 1988. Vandringer i Bergen. Bergen.

Forland, Astrid og Anders Haaland 1996. Universitetet i Bergens historie, Bd.1. Bergen.

Gran, Jens 1873. Skizzer af bergenske Forholde fra ældre og yngre Tid. Bergen.

Helland, Amund 1916. Topografisk-statistisk beskrivelse over Bergen, Bd.1–2. Kristiania.

Hartvedt, Gunnar Hagen 2003. Bergen byleksikon. Oslo.

Herteig, Asbjørn E. 1969. Kongers by og handels sete. Oslo.

Holberg, Ludvig 1920. Den Berømmelige Norske Handel-Stad Bergens Beskrivelse, 4. utg. Bergen.

Steen, Sverre 1970. Bergen, byen mellom fjellene. Bergen.

Welhaven, Elisabeth 1897. Fortællinger fra det gamle Bergen. Kristiania.